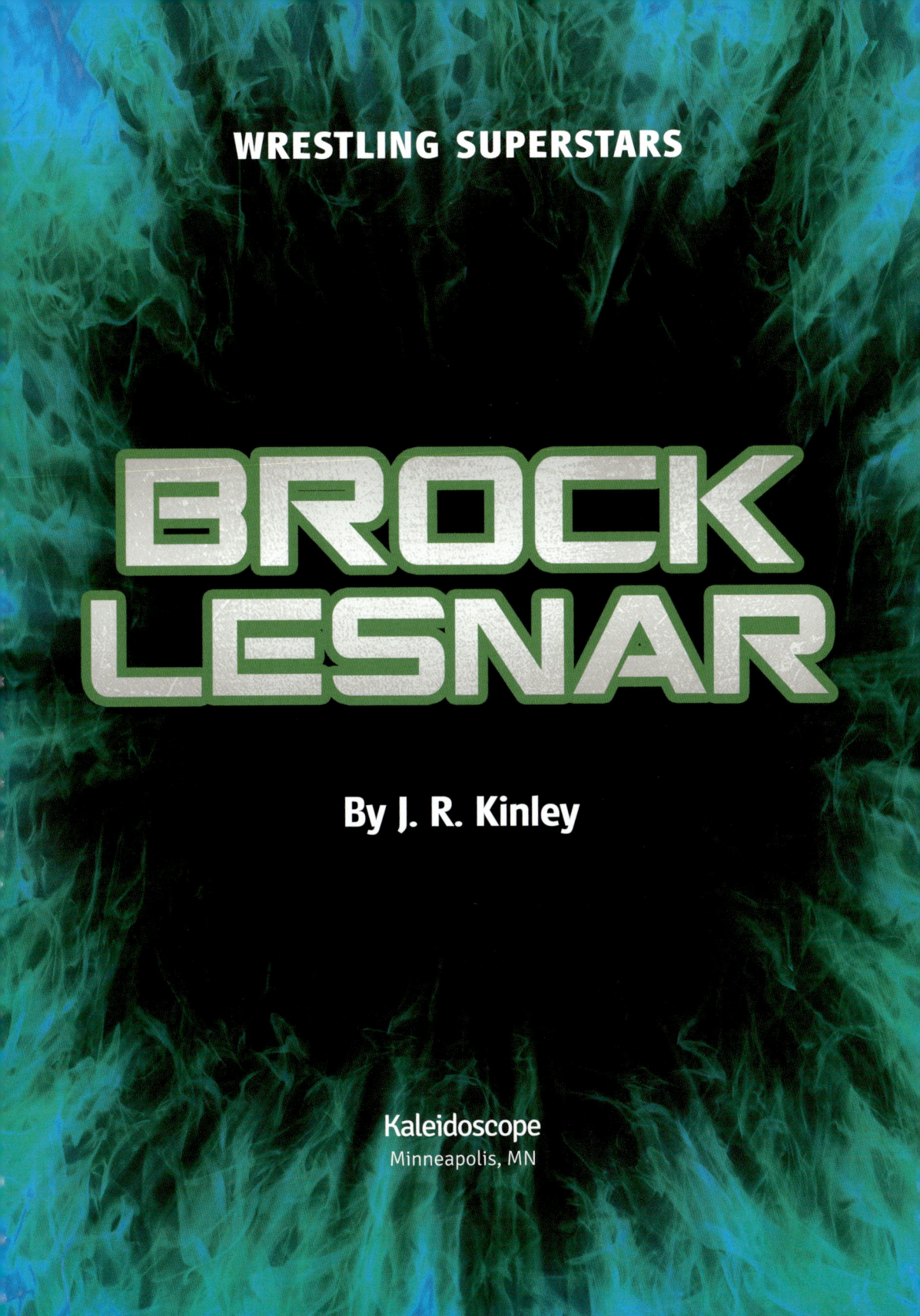

WRESTLING SUPERSTARS

BROCK LESNAR

By J. R. Kinley

Kaleidoscope
Minneapolis, MN

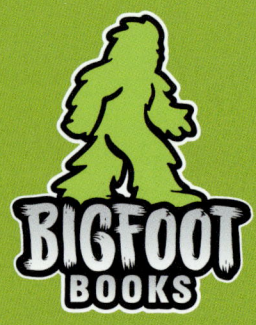

The Quest for Discovery Never Ends

. . . .

This edition first published in 2020 by Kaleidoscope Publishing, Inc.

No part of this publication may be reproduced in whole or in part without written permission of the publisher.

For information regarding permission, write to Kaleidoscope Publishing, Inc. 6012 Blue Circle Drive Minnetonka, MN 55343

Library of Congress Control Number 2019940195

ISBN
978-1-64519-086-8 (library bound)
978-1-64494-223-9 (paperback)
978-1-64519-187-2 (ebook)

Text copyright © 2020 by Kaleidoscope Publishing, Inc. All-Star Sports, Bigfoot Books, and associated logos are trademarks and/or registered trademarks of Kaleidoscope Publishing, Inc.

Printed in the United States of America.

Bigfoot lurks within one of the images in this book. It's up to you to find him!

TABLE OF CONTENTS

Chapter 1: The Next Big Thing **4**

Chapter 2: Dreaming of the Title **10**

Chapter 3: Bringing Pain **16**

Chapter 4: Return of the Beast **22**

Beyond the Book *28*

Research Ninja *29*

Further Resources *30*

Glossary *31*

Index *32*

Photo Credits *32*

About the Author *32*

CHAPTER 1

The Next Big Thing

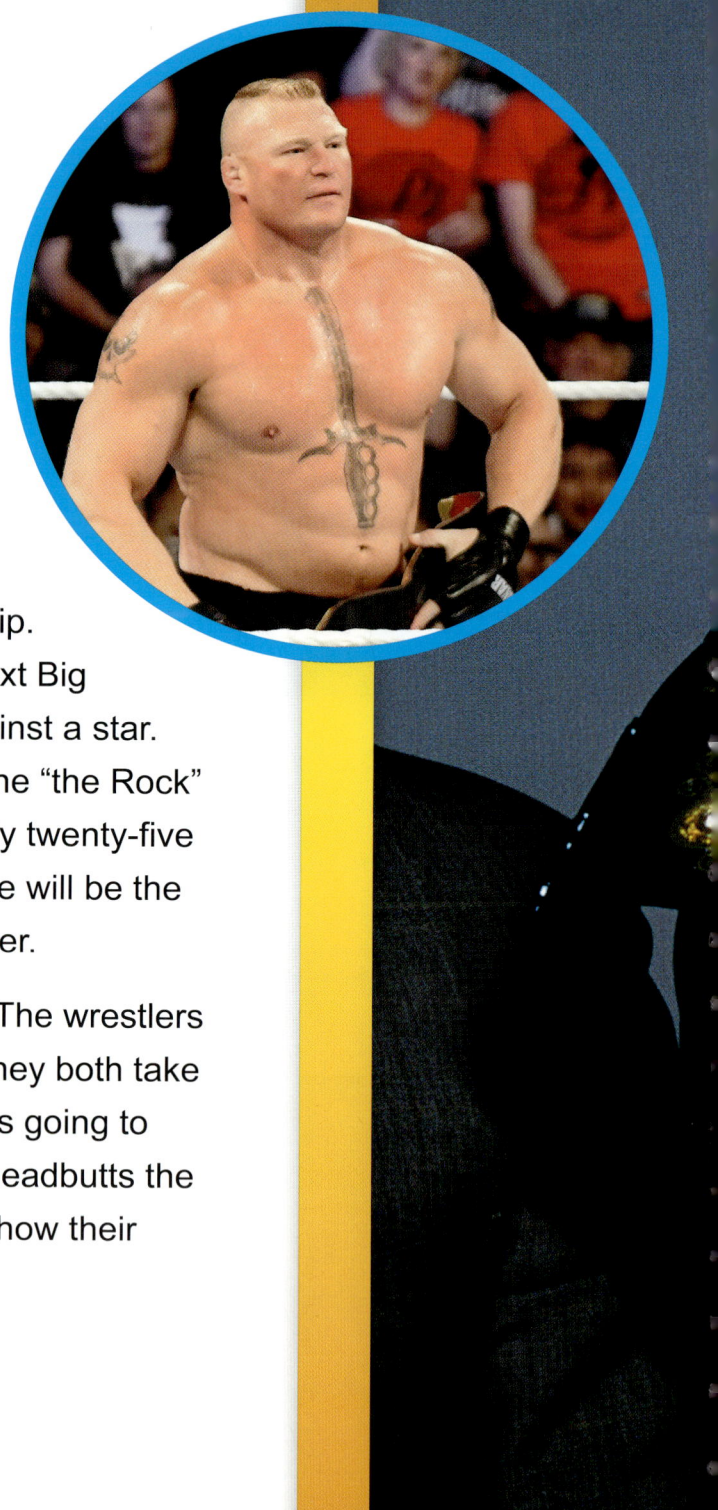

SummerSlam 2002 roars to a start. It's the World Wrestling Entertainment (WWE) title match. Brock Lesnar wants to win the championship. People call him the Next Big Thing. But he's up against a star. Lesnar is facing Dwayne "the Rock" Johnson. Lesnar is only twenty-five years old. If he wins, he will be the youngest champion ever.

The match begins. The wrestlers trade hard punches. They both take shots to the ribs. This is going to be a slugfest! Lesnar headbutts the Rock. Both wrestlers show their **brute** strength.

Brock Lesnar has been an intimidating force since he debuted with WWE in 2002.

WWE Champion Dwayne "the Rock" Johnson was a fierce opponent for a young Brock Lesnar.

Lesnar kicks the Rock through the ropes. They fight outside the ring. Then Lesnar throws the Rock back in.

Lesnar does a **suplex**. He flips the Rock over his head. The ref counts to two. But the Rock gets back up. He fires back with punches. Lesnar does a powerslam. He lifts the Rock and flips him over. Then, he slams him onto the mat. The Rock is down for two counts again.

Things start to turn around for the Rock. He punches Lesnar. He sends him to the mat with a **clothesline**. Then he holds Lesnar's legs in a painful lock. It seems like Lesnar might give in.

The Rock tries his finishing move. It's called the Rock Bottom. He slams Lesnar to the ground. The crowd chants, "Let's go, Lesnar." The Rock talks trash. But he gets caught by a BROCK Bottom! Lesnar uses the Rock's move against him!

FUN FACT
Brock Lesnar was featured on the cover of the *WWE 2K17* video game.

THE BEAST INCARNATE

Brock Lesnar is a big guy. He is often called "the Beast Incarnate." He is 6 feet, 3 inches (190 cm) tall. He weighs 286 pounds (130 kg). Lesnar has huge muscles. But he is still light on his feet. He can jump high and move fast.

Next, Lesnar tries his own finisher. It's called the F-5. He lifts the Rock onto his shoulders. He spins. He tries to throw the Rock to the ground. But the Rock lands on his feet. Lesnar tries again. This time, it works! Lesnar wins by a **pinfall**. He's the new champion. The torch passes to the Next Big Thing.

FUN FACT
A SummerSlam 2003 commercial showed Brock Lesnar performing an F-5 on a shark.

Brock Lesnar is known for his finishing move, the F-5.

CHAPTER 2

Dreaming of the Title

Brock Lesnar grew up in South Dakota. He lived on a farm. He would wake up early to milk the cows. The hayloft in the barn was like his jungle gym. He did push-ups and sit-ups. He wanted to be strong.

The school wrestling coach saw Lesnar's potential. Lesnar began **freestyle** wrestling. He didn't always win.

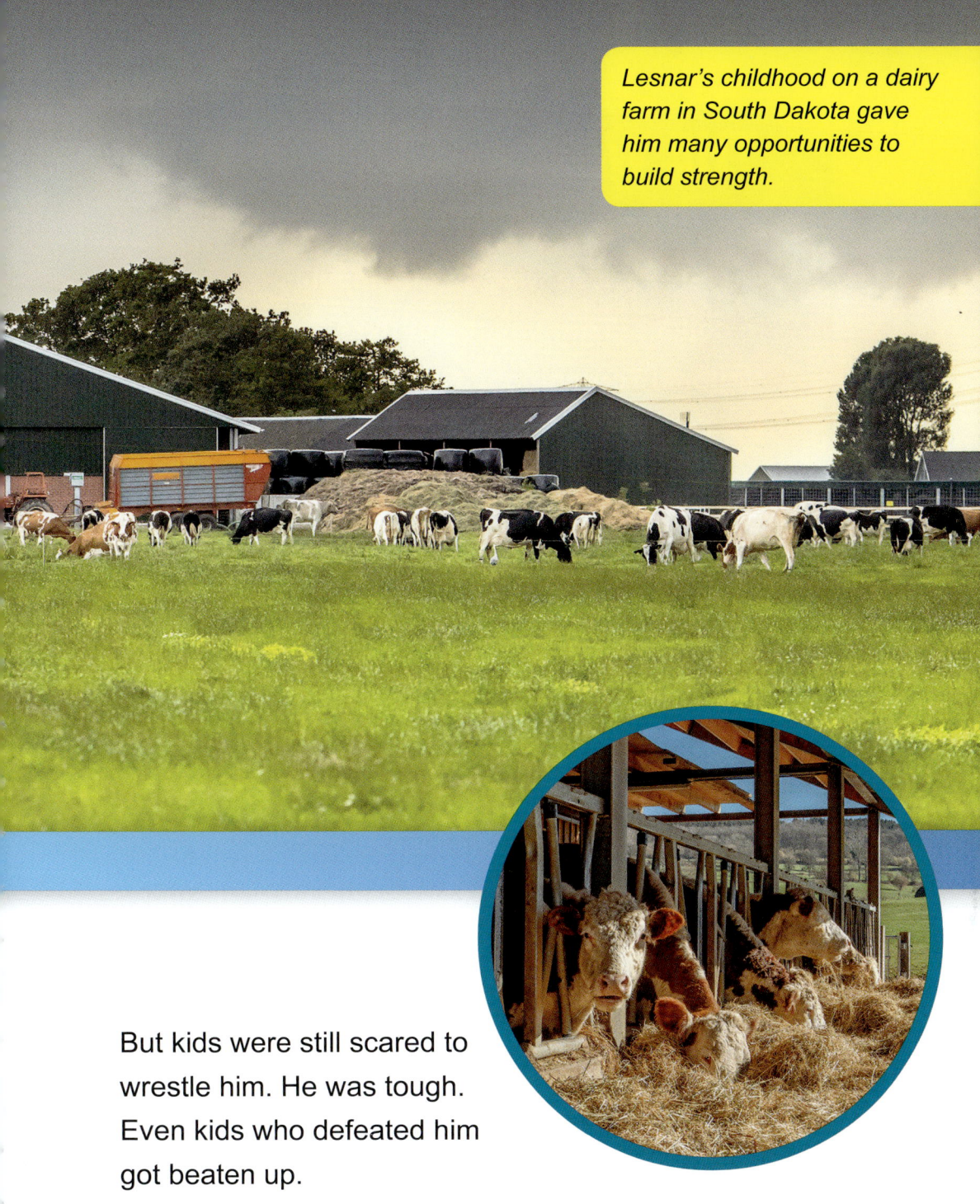

Lesnar's childhood on a dairy farm in South Dakota gave him many opportunities to build strength.

But kids were still scared to wrestle him. He was tough. Even kids who defeated him got beaten up.

Brock never won a state title in high school. But that drove him to improve. He wanted to be a college wrestler.

THE WRESTLING ELITE

Brock Lesnar was an elite freestyle wrestler. These wrestlers compete in college. They wrestle in the NCAA National Tournament. Some train for the Olympics. Others enter **promotions** like WWE. Lesnar chose to enter WWE.

He went to Bismarck State College. He won the junior college championship. Then he went to the University of Minnesota. He won twenty-four times in his junior year. He lost only twice. Lesnar was a finalist at the NCAA National Tournament.

People expected Lesnar to do well again the next year. And he wanted to win the title this time. *Sports Illustrated* interviewed him. He said, "It takes more than talent. It's about heart and desire, and I want it more than anyone."

Soon, Lesnar got his chance. He faced his rival, Wes Hand. It was the final round of the tournament. They wrestled for the title. The regular match time ended. But they were tied. The match went into overtime.

Brock Lesnar got his start by freestyle wrestling at school.

The overtime round is two minutes long. The first wrestler to score a point wins. Lesnar and Hand traded shots. But time ran out and neither scored. They went into another overtime round. Lesnar won a coin flip. He chose to start from the down position. This meant Hand would start out in control. Lesnar would try to escape within thirty seconds. If he did, he would win. The whistle blew. Hand wrapped his arms around Lesnar's waist.

They grappled. Hand got a bloody nose. They took a break. Then the wrestlers went back to the circle. Fourteen seconds remained. Lesnar escaped with nine seconds left. He got the point. Lesnar jogged around the circle to celebrate. He won the national title!

The ref raised Lesnar's hand in the air. Lesnar thought, "I did it. I finally did it."

FUN FACT
Lesnar started wrestling when he was five years old.

Lesnar's NCAA National Tournament match against Wes Hand was a huge moment in his career.

CHAPTER 3

Bringing Pain

Brock Lesnar does more than just wrestle. For a while, he competed in **mixed martial arts** (MMA). His time doing MMA taught him new moves. He brought them back to WWE. One of these moves is the Kimura Lock.

One of the dangerous moves that Lesnar brought back from his time competing in mixed martial arts was the Kimura Lock.

The Kimura Lock is one of Lesnar's signature moves. These are the moves a wrestler is known for. Pro wrestlers train and practice. They learn how to avoid seriously hurting each other. They know how to perform dangerous moves. But sometimes wrestlers are still hurt. The Kimura Lock once broke Triple H's arm.

Lesnar trains hard and practices his signature moves.

FUN FACT
Lesnar can do an impressive backflip move called the Shooting Star Press.

In 2012, John Cena and Lesnar faced off. Lesnar had just returned to WWE. Lesnar trapped Cena's upper arm. He held it in a Kimura Lock. The Kimura is a shoulder lock. It is a type of **submission hold**. It can cause serious injury. Wrestlers need to know when to **tap out** of this hold. If they don't tap out in time, they may get hurt. It could take six months to recover from an injury.

Cena managed to escape. Lesnar had injured his arm, though. In the end, Cena beat Lesnar. But not without paying a painful price.

LESNAR'S F-5 FINISHER

Opponent lifted onto shoulders

Overhead spin

Opponent slammed to the mat face-first

Lesnar faced John Cena again in 2014. He used the F-5 to get back at him. This is his finishing move. *F5* is a rating that used to be given to powerful tornadoes. First, Lesnar lifted Cena onto his shoulders. Then he spun him. He threw Cena down to the mat. The F-5 won him the match. It has won him many other matches over the years.

Moves like the Kimura Lock and the F-5 help Lesnar win big matches and titles.

CHAPTER 4

Return of the Beast

After college, Lesnar trained for WWE. He worked hard and performed well. In 2002, he was called up. He started on *Raw*. He racked up wins. He earned big titles.

In 2004, Lesnar took a break from wrestling. He tried playing football. He signed with the Minnesota Vikings. He went to training camp. He didn't make the final cut. But he played in the preseason. He even suplexed a player from another team.

After that, Lesnar wrestled in Japan. He won the international title. He went on to compete in MMA.

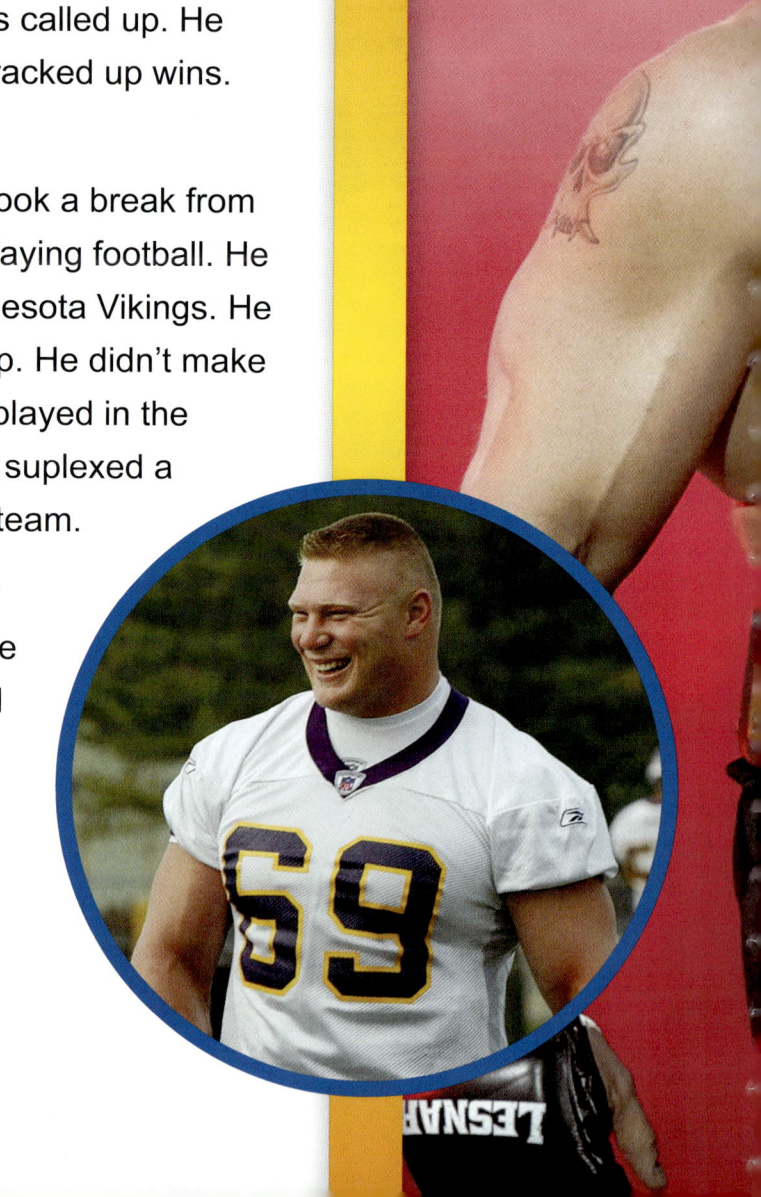

Lesnar has won many belts during his career.

In April 2012, Lesnar returned to WWE. His fans were happy he came back. He walked into the arena. The crowd erupted with cheers. But his opponents must have been nervous. The Beast had returned. His new MMA skills seemed dangerous. Those matches had been bloody.

But Lesnar had his eyes on the Undertaker. The Undertaker had a perfect record at WrestleMania. No one had ever beat him there. Lesnar faced him at WrestleMania in 2014. Everyone thought the Undertaker would win again. Lesnar would be another name on the long list of losers. But Lesnar pinned him. The crowd was shocked. The Undertaker's winning streak was over.

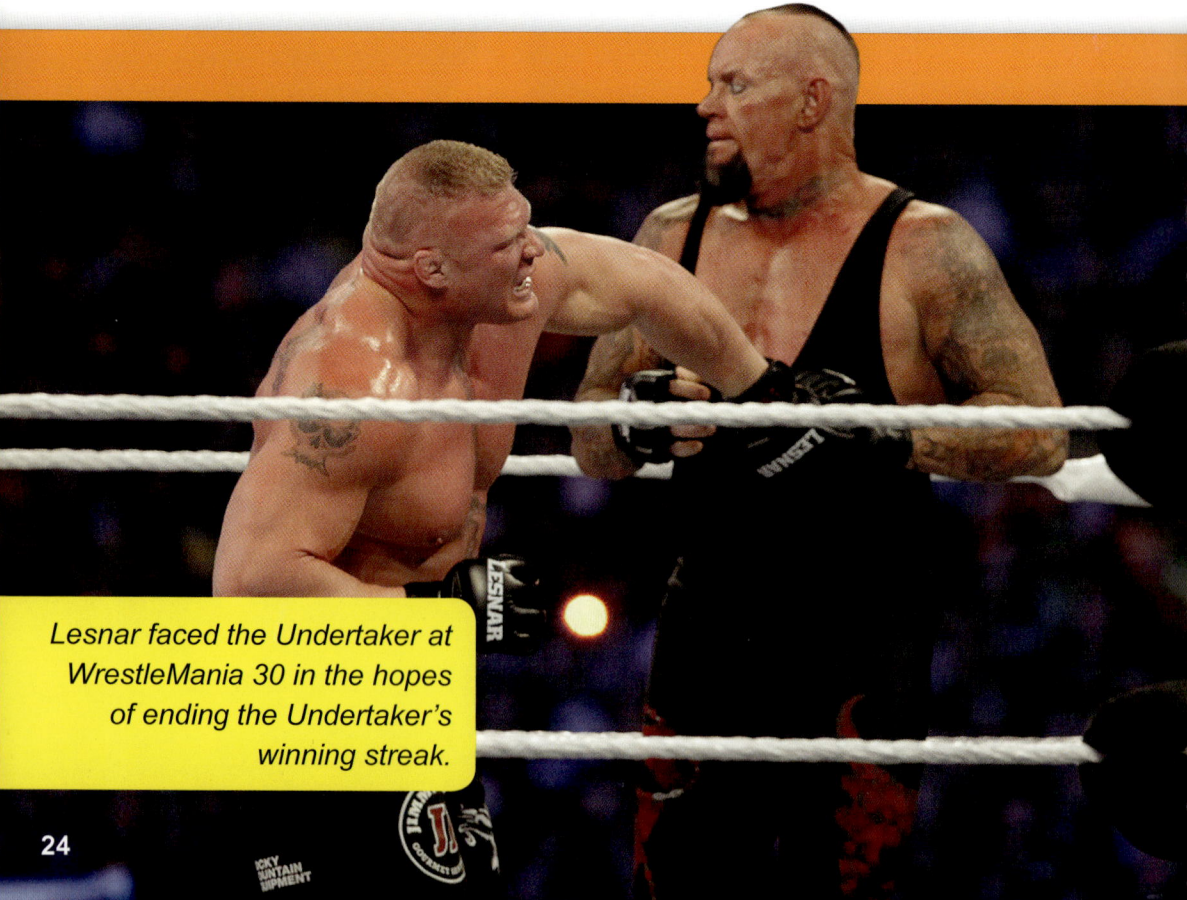

Lesnar faced the Undertaker at WrestleMania 30 in the hopes of ending the Undertaker's winning streak.

CAREER HIGHLIGHTS

2002

March 18, 2002
Lesnar debuts on the WWE main roster.

June 23, 2002
Lesnar wins the WWE King of the Ring tournament.

2003

August 25, 2002
Lesnar beats the Rock to win his first WWE Championship. At age twenty-five, he is the youngest in history to win it.

2003
Lesnar claims two WWE World Champion title wins.

2007

2005–2007
Lesnar wrestles with promotions in Japan and wins an international title.

2011

2008–2011
Lesnar fights with UFC and wins the heavyweight title.

2012

April 2, 2012
Lesnar returns to WWE.

2014

April 6, 2014
Lesnar ends the Undertaker's winning streak at WrestleMania 30.

August 17, 2014
Lesnar defeats John Cena for his fourth WWE Championship.

2017

April 2, 2017, and November 2, 2018
Lesnar claims the WWE Universal Championship.

Four months later, Brock Lesnar faced John Cena for the WWE Championship. Lesnar took Cena to "Suplex City." Lesnar used this phrase to describe his attack. He hit sixteen German suplexes against Cena.

Then he finished Cena off. He used the F-5 to pin him. Lesnar claimed the title.

Since then, Lesnar has won two Universal Championships. He is a WWE Superstar.

FUN FACT
Brock Lesnar is red-green color-blind.

Lesnar is known to take opponents to "Suplex City."

BEYOND THE BOOK

After reading the book, it's time to think about what you learned. Try the following exercises to jumpstart your ideas.

THINK

THAT'S NEWS TO ME. What types of sources might you be able to find on Brock Lesnar's MMA career? How could each kind of source be useful in its own way?

CREATE

SHARPEN YOUR RESEARCH SKILLS. Brock Lesnar does a lot of weight training to develop his muscles and strength. Where could you go in your school or community, or who could you talk to, to learn more about weight training? Write a paragraph describing these next steps for research.

SHARE

WHAT'S YOUR OPINION? The text states that when Brock Lesnar returned to WWE in 2012, his opponents must have been nervous. Do you agree with this? What information from the book supports this opinion? Share your opinion and evidence with a friend. Does your friend find your argument convincing?

GROW

DRAWING CONNECTIONS. Draw a diagram that shows how professional wrestling relates to martial arts. How does learning about martial arts help you to better understand professional wrestling?

RESEARCH NINJA

Visit www.ninjaresearcher.com/0868 to learn how to take your research skills and book report writing to the next level!

RESEARCH

DIGITAL LITERACY TOOLS

SEARCH LIKE A PRO
Learn about how to use search engines to find useful websites.

FACT OR FAKE?
Discover how you can tell a trusted website from an untrustworthy resource.

TEXT DETECTIVE
Explore how to zero in on the information you need most.

SHOW YOUR WORK
Research responsibly— learn how to cite sources.

WRITE

GET TO THE POINT
Learn how to express your main ideas.

PLAN OF ATTACK
Learn prewriting exercises and create an outline.

DOWNLOADABLE REPORT FORMS

Further Resources

BOOKS

Black, Jake. *WWE Ultimate Superstar Guide*. WWE / DK Publishing / Penguin Random House, 2018.

Scheff, Matt. *Brock Lesnar*. Bearport, 2015.

Scheff, Matt. *Pro Wrestling's Greatest Rivalries*. Abdo Publishing, 2017.

WEBSITES

Factsurfer.com gives you a safe, fun way to find more information.

1. Go to www.factsurfer.com.
2. Enter "Brock Lesnar" into the search box and click 🔍.
3. Select your book cover to see a list of related websites.

Glossary

brute: Brute strength is physical or savage. Lesnar and the Rock showed their brute strength during their match.

clothesline: For a clothesline, a wrestler extends an arm and hits the opponent in the neck area to knock him or her down. Brock Lesnar used a clothesline on the Rock.

freestyle: Freestyle wrestling is a type of wrestling that is usually done in schools. Brock Lesnar wrestled freestyle in high school and college.

mixed martial arts: In mixed martial arts, fighters use different combat styles, like kickboxing and karate. Brock Lesnar brought mixed martial arts moves back with him to WWE.

pinfall: A pinfall is when a wrestler holds an opponent's shoulders to the mat for an official count to three, winning the match. Brock Lesnar won the match by a pinfall.

promotions: Promotions are companies or groups that organize matches and shows for sports like boxing and wrestling. WWE is one of many wrestling promotions.

submission hold: A submission hold is a hold or lock that uses pressure on a part of an opponent's body. The wrestler tapped out of the submission hold.

suplex: For a suplex, a wrestler locks his or her arms around an opponent's waist, then throws him or her backward to the mat. Lesnar leaned back and took Cena down with a suplex.

tap out: To tap out is to give in to a submission hold. In a painful arm lock, the wrestler may tap out to be released.

Index

career timeline, 25
Cena, John, 19, 21, 25, 26–27
championships, 4, 8, 12, 25, 26–27

F-5, 8, 20, 21, 27
freestyle wrestling, 10–12

Hand, Wes, 12, 14

Johnson, Dwayne "the Rock," 4, 7–8, 25

Kimura Lock, 16–17, 19

Minnesota Vikings, 22
MMA, 16, 22, 24

NCAA, 12

suplexes, 7, 22, 26

UFC, 25
Undertaker, the, 24, 25

WWE, 4, 12, 16, 19, 22, 24, 25, 26–27
WWE 2K17, 7

PHOTO CREDITS

The images in this book are reproduced through the courtesy of: Don Feria/AP Images, front cover (Brock Lesnar); Valeriy Lebedev/Shutterstock Images, front cover (background); John Palmer/MediaPunch/IPX/AP Images, pp. 3, 20, 21; Jackie Brown/Newscom, p. 4; Simon Galloway/EMPICS/PA Images/Getty Images, pp. 4–5, 25 (Brock Lesnar); Marc Serota/WWE/AP Images, p. 6; charnsitr/Shutterstock Images, p. 7; Matt Roberts/Zuma Press/Icon Sportswire, pp. 9, 24; Rudmer Zwerver/Shutterstock Images, pp. 10–11; itsajoop/Shutterstock Images, p. 11; JoeSAPhotos/Shutterstock Images, p. 13; Bill Greenblatt/UPI Photo Service/Newscom, pp. 14–15; guruXOX/Shutterstock Images, pp. 16–17; Jim Mone/AP Images, pp. 18–19, 22; Pressmaster/Shutterstock Images, p. 19; Don Feria/WWE/AP Images, pp. 22–23, 30; Red Line Editorial, p. 25 (timeline); Chad Matthew Carlson/Sports Illustrated/Set Number: X161332 TK1/Getty Images, pp. 26–27.

ABOUT THE AUTHOR

J. R. Kinley is a writer and artist. She is part of a wrestling family from Ohio in one of the top wrestling regions in the nation. Her husband, Shaun Kinley, former NCAA wrestler at The Ohio State University, coaches at the nationally ranked St. Edward High School. Together, they operate Kinley Studio.